JENNIFER SCHAEFER

# I KNOW GOD, BUT DO I KNOW

God?

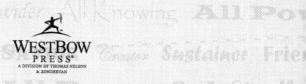

WESTBOW
PRESS®
A DIVISION OF THOMAS NELSON
& ZONDERVAN

WestBow Press books may be ordered through booksellers or by contacting:

WestBow Press
A Division of Thomas Nelson & Zondervan
1663 Liberty Drive
Bloomington, IN 47403
www.westbowpress.com
844-714-3454

Because of the dynamic nature of the Internet, any web addresses or
links contained in this book may have changed since publication and
may no longer be valid. The views expressed in this work are solely those
of the author and do not necessarily reflect the views of the publisher,
and the publisher hereby disclaims any responsibility for them.

Any people depicted in stock imagery provided by Getty Images are
models, and such images are being used for illustrative purposes only.
Certain stock imagery © Getty Images.

Scripture taken from the King James Version of the Bible.

ISBN: 978-1-6642-5402-2 (sc)
ISBN: 978-1-6642-5404-6 (hc)
ISBN: 978-1-6642-5403-9 (e)

Library of Congress Control Number: 2021925641

Print information available on the last page.

WestBow Press rev. date: 06/14/2022

# Contents

# Introduction

I know God, but do I *know* God? The question could be asked, "I know God—as in, I have accepted Him as my personal Lord and Savior; but do I know God—as in, who He is and how that relates to me personally?" On the other hand, the question could be asked, "I know God—as in, I know all about who He is; but do I know God—as in, have I accepted Him as my personal Lord and Savior?" I remember a song that was sung at many of the revival services I attended as a child. It said, "You may know a lot about Him, but do you really know Him?" How sad it would be for someone to read God's Word and to know who God is, but never know Him as his or her personal Lord and Savior.

I grew up in a Christian home. I have attended church faithfully all my life. I have attended Sunday school, Christian school, and a Christian college. I have even worked in the ministry. Though none of these things could ever save me, one would probably think, knowing my background, that I do not only know Him as my personal Lord and Savior but that I should know a lot about God and who He is to me personally. At the young age of twelve, I asked Jesus to save me, and I know that He did. I have never battled with assurance of my salvation. However, through the trials and tribulations of my life, I must admit that, although I know Him as my personal Lord and Savior, I have not always acknowledged the truth about who He is to me personally.

Viewing God through the circumstances of life will always lead you to a false understanding of who God is entirely. It is through the precious promises that God gives to us in His Holy Word, where we can truly learn of who God is to us personally. The more we get to know Him, the more precious He becomes to us on a personal level.

It may be somewhat difficult to understand. You see, I could write out all the attributes—or characteristics—of God and have a head knowledge of what those attributes are, but there have been times in my life when I have not really believed them to be true or personally applied them to my life. When you truly put God first in your life, allow Him to organize and prioritize your life according to His standards, and you experience the sweetness of walking with Him and spending time with Him in prayer, the Christian life becomes something entirely different. Salvation is so much more than just a ticket into heaven. To truly live a victorious and fulfilled Christian life, one must also know God!

# Section 1:

## How Do I Know God?

This book is primarily intended for believers. It is my desire to help Christians fully embrace their personal relationships with God and get to know God on a more personal level while still here on this earth. However, if you do not Know God as your personal Lord and Savior, a relationship with Him cannot and will not ever exist. May I take a moment and share with you how you can know, for sure, that you know God as your personal Lord and Savior?

Experiencing salvation for yourself is easiest put into three biblical truths. I often hear them referred to as the ABCs of salvation:

1. You must *admit* that you are lost and in need of a Savior.
2. You must *believe* that Christ died for your sins and rose victorious.
3. You must *call* on Him to save you.

These are not ideas that I have made up on my own or have based on standards that I have created. No, these truths are laid out in God's Holy Word, which is the final authority and the roadmap for the redemption that God has sacrificed on our behalf.

# The Three Biblical Truths of Salvation

# Admit That You Are Lost
# and in Need of a Savior

How can you conclude your need for a Savior if you do not first understand that you are lost? What must you be saved from? The Bible clearly states that you and I are sinners, and each of us has fallen short of God's expectations. "For all have sinned and come short of the glory of God" (Romans 3:23).

We are all born with a sin nature, and therefore, from birth, we immediately fall short of the privilege to enter into the presence of our holy, or sinless, Creator. "As it is written, There is none righteous, no, not one" (Romans 3:10).

You may then ask, "What is sin?" Sin can be best described as any act of disobedience against God, which is also clearly defined in God's Word. "For by the law is the knowledge of sin" (Romans 3:20b).

In fact, the Bible also tells us that the law is written on the very hearts of mankind, in the form of our conscience. The conscience gives us the ability to determine between right and wrong, but because of our sinful natures, we can also excuse the conscience. "Which shew the work of the law written in their hearts, their conscience also bearing witness, and their thoughts the mean while accusing or else excusing one another" (Romans 2:15).

The Bible also clearly confirms that there is a wage or payment that must be made for our sins, and there is no question that one day we will all face this payment in the form of death itself. The question is, where will you go one second after death? "For the wages of sin is death; but the gift of God is eternal life through Jesus Christ our Lord" (Romans 6:23).

If you have never accepted God's payment for your sins, then you are destined to pay for your own sins in a place of torment, separated from God for all eternity. "And these shall go away into everlasting punishment: but the righteous into life eternal" (Matthew 25:46).

# Believe That Christ Died for Your Sins and Rose Victorious

Praise God, He has given us an ultimatum and a free will to choose whether or not to accept the payment that He made for us and to avoid the awful punishment that our sins require. "For God so loved the world, that he gave his only begotten Son, that whosoever believeth in him should not perish, but have everlasting life" (John 3:16).

In this selfless act of pure love, death, hell, and the grave were conquered so that we may have not only an escape from the torment that awaits but also an avenue for a personal relationship with God Himself. If we believe and accept this priceless gift—which is the death and shed blood of God's only Son on the cross—as the only acceptable payment for our sins, we are promised a home in heaven with God for all eternity. "Let not your heart be troubled: ye believe in God, believe also in me. In my Father's house are many mansions: if it were not so, I would have told you. I go to prepare a place for you. And if I go and prepare a place for you, I will come again, and receive you unto myself; that where I am, there ye may be also" (John 14:1–3).

There is truly no greater love than giving one's life for another. "Greater love hath no man than this, that a man lay down his life for his friends" (John 15:13). However, it is the shed blood of Jesus, who is sinless and perfect, that is the only acceptable sacrifice for the sins of all mankind. "But God commendeth His love toward us, in that, while we were yet sinners, Christ died for us" (Romans 5:8).

His sacrifice was much greater than just death alone. While on the cross, Jesus bore our sins and carried our sorrows. "Who his own self bare our sins in his own body on the tree, that we, being dead to sins, should live unto righteousness: by whose stripes ye are healed" (1 Peter 2:24).

On the cross, Jesus took on the sinful ugliness of mankind. In exchange, He gave us freedom from our sins. There is truly no greater picture of pure love and forgiveness than Christ's sacrifice for us.

It is also important to know that there is only one way, not multiple ways, to heaven. "Jesus saith unto him, I am the way, the truth, and the life: no man cometh unto the Father, but by me" (John 14:6).

It is not through the acceptance of what Jesus did for us on the cross plus the good works that we try to perform in our own flesh. It is not through the acceptance of what Jesus did for us on the cross plus being baptized. It is not through the acceptance of what Jesus did for us on the cross plus … you fill in the blank. It is through Jesus *alone* that we are saved. "Not by works of righteousness which we have done, but according to his mercy he saved us, by the washing of regeneration, and renewing of the Holy Ghost" (Titus 3:5).

And, of course, without His triumphant resurrection, His death on the cross would have been completely in vain. "For if we believe that Jesus died and rose again, even so them also which sleep in Jesus will God bring with Him" (1 Thessalonians 4:14).

# Call on Jesus to Save You

$O$nce you have admitted your lost condition and you believe that salvation is in Christ alone through the shed blood of Jesus and His victorious resurrection, you must call upon Him to save you. "That if thou shalt confess with thy mouth the Lord Jesus, and shalt believe in thine heart that God hath raised him from the dead, thou shalt be saved" (Romans 10:9). Salvation is honestly that simple! "For whosoever shall call upon the name of the Lord shall be saved" (Romans 10:13).

God loves us so much that He sent His Son to die for us, but did you also know that He seeks us? "For the Son of man is come to seek and to save that which was lost" (Luke 19:10). He seeks us! He does not force us. He does not push us. He seeks us! It is His desire for all to be saved. "The Lord is not slack concerning his promise, as some men count slackness; but is longsuffering to us-ward, not willing that any should perish, but that *all* should come to repentance" (2 Peter 3:9).

My friend, if you have never taken this step, I strongly urge you to accept Him as your personal Lord and Savior. This is the single most-important decision you will ever make in your lifetime, and I can personally guarantee that you will never regret making the decision to accept Christ as your Savior.

# The Greatest Story Ever Told

by Adam Morgan

Sin grips the heart within
a curse on fallen men.
This pride and selfishness we hold inside.
Though we were all condemned,
We had a loving friend who came to save us.
He lived a perfect life
And gave the blind their sight,
Fulfilled the things foretold by prophecy.
He humbly took His cross
And died to save the lost,
Their sins forgiven.
The greatest story ever told is of this Jesus,
How He came to earth to rescue sinful men,
Sent from the Father up above
To sacrifice in love and take our place
And give unending grace.
This Son of God who gave His life
And took the grave
Obeyed His Father's will despite the cost.
But death could not contain
His pow'r, His love, His grace, for He is risen!
The greatest story ever told is of this Jesus,
How He came to earth to rescue sinful men,
Sent from the Father up above
To sacrifice in love and take our place
And give unending grace.
The greatest story ever told is of this Jesus.[1]

# My Personal Salvation Testimony

As I mentioned before, I grew up in a Christian home. I was brought up in church. I was taught about the Bible before I could even read. I remember as a child, saying a prayer of salvation on two separate occasions. Through these two experiences, I received a head knowledge but not a heart knowledge of salvation. It was not until I was twelve years old that God began to work in my heart and show me how lost I truly was. In my own eyes, I had never committed any heinous crimes. I had never done anything outrageously "wrong," but that didn't matter. I was still just as lost as a person sitting on death row for committing murder.

You see, God does not look at a person's outward appearance; He looks at the heart. "But the Lord said unto Samuel, Look not on his countenance, or on the height of his stature; because I have refused him: for the Lord seeth not as man seeth; for man looketh on the outward appearance, but the Lord looketh on the heart" (1 Samuel 16:7). Every human is born with a sinful nature and has a void in his or her heart that can only be filled by God. "Behold, I was shapen in iniquity; and in sin did my mother conceive me" (Psalms 51:5).

I could repeat how to be saved step by step, but until I admitted my lost condition, I did not really know Christ as my personal Lord and Savior. I remember being under tremendous conviction and being fearful that the rapture would take place and that my entire family would be raptured out, and I would be left all alone. I grabbed my mom and told her that I must talk to her. We went to my bedroom, and I told her what was bothering me. I asked her, "How do you know for sure that you are saved?" I remember her telling me, "Jennifer, only you know in your heart if you are saved or not."

It was at that moment that I admitted I was lost. I admitted that I needed a Savior, and I accepted Christ into my heart as payment for my sins. I remember there was much fear in my heart before that moment, but once Christ came into my heart to save me, I felt a peace that passes all understanding. "Therefore being justified by faith, we have peace with God through our Lord Jesus Christ: By whom also we have access by faith into this grace wherein we stand, and rejoice in hope of the glory of God" (Romans 5:1–2).

# Blessed Assurance

*by Fanny J. Crosby*

Blessed assurance, Jesus is mine!
Oh, what a foretaste of glory divine!
Heir of salvation, purchase of God,
Born of His Spirit, washed in His blood.
Perfect submission, perfect delight,
Visions of rapture now burst on my sight;
Angels descending, bring from above
Echoes of mercy, whispers of love.
Perfect submission, all is at rest,
I in my Savior am happy and blest;
Watching and waiting, looking above,
Filled with His goodness, lost in His love.
This is my story, this is my song,
Praising my Savior all the day long;
This is my story, this is my song,
Praising my Savior all the day long.

# My Burden and Desire

Because I grew up in a Christian home, I have a special burden for those who have also grown up in Christian homes and who may know all about God but who do not truly know Him. It is not my desire to make anyone doubt his or her salvation, but it is my desire to alert those who only have a head knowledge of God that they must experience the heart knowledge to have a relationship with Christ. It truly breaks my heart to know that there are numerous children who grow up in Christian homes and have "religion" but who do not have personal relationships with God.

I am also truly blessed, having been saved at an early age, not to have borne the burden of sin for so long. I have heard many testimonies of people who God brought out of the very depths of sin and lives of pure evil, to God be the glory! I have also heard some Christians, who were saved earlier in their lives, say they wished they had a more "dramatic" testimony. But if you ask any person who God has gloriously saved from the very pit of hell, they will tell you no, you do not wish that. To be spared early from a horrible life of sin and regret is a blessing I do not ever want to take for granted.

# Growing in His Grace and Knowledge

*P*utting your faith and trust in the saving power of the blood of Jesus is merely the first step to having a relationship with God. He not only wants to save your soul from an eternal separation from Him but He also has a specific plan and purpose for your life.

One of the evidences of salvation is a true change in your heart and life. For what God has done for us, giving our lives to Christ to use as He desires is quite a small sacrifice. "I beseech you therefore, brethren, by the mercies of God, that ye present your bodies a living sacrifice, holy, acceptable unto God, which is your reasonable service" (Romans 12:1–2). To learn of His plan and perfect will for your life, you must grow in Christ. A good way to grow in your Christian walk is to learn about who God is and who He is to you personally.

# Section 2: But Do I Really Know God?

Who is God? A relationship with Him must now be built. It cannot be developed overnight or instantaneously. Once you accept Christ as your Savior, it is His desire to develop a relationship with you on an individual basis. Isn't that amazing? God not only sacrificed Himself for you and me, but He wants to know you and me personally. Wow, mind-blowing!

Charles Spurgeon once said, "Nearness to God brings likeness to God. The more you see God, the more of God will be seen in you." It is important in our Christian lives to get to the point where we recognize that God is ultimately all that we need. His Word holds the answer to every question, the solution to every problem, and the comfort for every heartache. While on this earth, we will never run out of opportunities to learn more about Him and ways to grow closer to Him. Though I personally have many more lessons to learn and will have many more opportunities to grow closer to Him, I believe He has placed it on my heart to share a few of my personal experiences in which He has helped me to grow closer to Him and to realize that, in fact, He is all I will ever need.

Elisabeth Elliot put it this way, "The recognition of who God is, is a Lifelong Process." In the chapters ahead, I would like to share with you a few of the attributes, or characteristics, of God that have really been a comfort and help to me. My prayer is that they will be a help and comfort to you and will encourage you to draw closer to your Savior. We are all different, and each of our circumstances are unique—but praise God, He never changes. "Jesus Christ the same yesterday, and to day, and for ever" (Hebrews 13:8).

If He said it, you can count on it! The scriptures are filled with God's wonderful promises that we can and must live by every day to have a victorious Christian life.

# Fearfully and Wonderfully Made

# God Is My Creator

God is the Creator of the world and all that is in the world (Genesis 1:1–31), which includes all of mankind. "So God created man in his own image, in the image of God created he him; male and female created he them" (Genesis 1:27).

Have you ever just sat and thought about the intricacies of the human body? God thought of absolutely everything. The human body is so complex and truly amazing!

Not only did He create us, but the Bible says that He knew us before we were created. "Before I formed thee in the belly I knew thee" (Jeremiah 1:5a). He knows us even better than we know ourselves. He knows every detail about us and still chooses to love and value us. "But even the very hairs of your head are all numbered. Fear not therefore: ye are of more value than many sparrows" (Luke 12:7). We do not truly know what love is until we know God. The Bible says that God is love! "God is love; and he that dwelleth in love dwelleth in God, and God in him" (1 John 4:16b).

There is no such thing as an "accident" when a human life is involved. Every human being has a purpose, and God has a plan for every life. Have you ever had one of those days, though—you know, when you feel that you are flawed, less-than, or unacceptable? Maybe you have an insecurity that has always plagued you. We all struggle from time to time with a lack of confidence. Satan likes to attack the mind. That is why we must fill our minds with the Word of God. I like the way Greg Locke put it. He said, "Satan's target is your mind, and his weapons are lies. Fill your mind with the Word of God." That is the only way we can have victory over the lies, or fiery darts, that Satan shoots into our minds.

"I will praise thee; for I am fearfully and wonderfully made: marvelous are thy works; and that my soul knoweth right well." (Psalm 139:14). I am fearfully and wonderfully made. You are fearfully and wonderfully made. God made you just the way that you are; you are unique. You are one of a kind, and you are very special. *Marvelous* literally means, "causing great wonder, extraordinary." Think about that for a while! Every human being is fashioned exclusively by God Himself. If we had multiple versions of the same person, with the exact same looks, talents, and personalities, that would become old and mondain very quickly, wouldn't it? Each of us is an individual with unique qualities, talents, and personalities.

Insecurities, however, are tactics that Satan uses to attack even the most victorious of Christians. Like I said before, everyone is different. We have those who are quiet and reserved, vocal and outgoing, excitable and upbeat, calm and tranquil, and so on. Somehow, Satan always seems to find a way to creep his way into our minds and tell us that we are not what we should be or that we were made a specific way as a punishment or a source of torture. This is so very untrue! God says, "For I know the thoughts that I think toward you, saith the Lord, thoughts of peace, and not of evil, to give you an expected end. Then shall ye call upon me, and ye shall go and pray unto me, and I will hearken unto you. And ye shall seek me, and find me, when ye shall search for me with all your heart" (Jeremiah 29:11).

In many ways, God uses these insecurities to draw us closer to Him and to make us more like Him. As Christians, these are two of the things we should want most in our lives. God's Word says, "Be careful for nothing; but in every thing by prayer and supplication with thanksgiving let your requests be made known unto God. And the peace of God, which passeth all understanding, shall keep your hearts and minds through Christ Jesus. Finally, brethren, whatsoever things are pure, whatsoever things are lovely, whatsoever things are of good report; if there be any virtue, and if there be any praise, think on these things. Those things, which ye have both learned, and received, and heard, and seen in me, do: and the God of peace shall be with you" (Philippians 4:6–9).

When applying these verses to an insecurity, God is telling us not to be anxious or worried about such things. Unfortunately, most insecurities tend to cause a great deal of anxiety and distress in our lives. Instead of worrying about them, we are to pray about them and be thankful for them. We are to cling to the truths that God gives us in His Word and meditate on those truths. This is a perfect example of how you can draw closer to Him. When we pray, we are talking to God; when we read the Bible, He is talking to us. Like Clyde Box once said, "Open the Bible, and you have opened the mind of God!"

Take your insecurities to the Lord; trust Him to help you overcome them and become the victorious Christian that He desires you to be.

# My Own Personal Experience of Insecurities

I can give you two great examples of insecurities in my own life. One I have learned to overcome, and God has given me the victory in this area. The other ... well, let's just say I may struggle with it for my entire life. Sometimes I ask God, "Why? Why am I different," or "Why am I like this?" I may not ever know the real reason why until I get to heaven, but what I do know is that I must turn to scripture. I am fearfully and wonderfully made, and I must hold on to that truth or Satan will try to sell me one of his lies. Honestly, if this insecurity consistently keeps me close to God, then I can, in fact, be thankful for it because it continuously draws me closer to Him.

The first example is the birthmark on my arm. I know many people are born with birthmarks, and they do not seem to be that big of a deal nowadays. But when I was a child, I seemed to be the only kid around with a mark on my skin. I got asked about it all the time. "Did you fall and scrape your arm? Is that mud on your arm?" And, of course, when I got older, children had no problem with coming right out and informing me of a large brown thing on my arm and asking me what it was. I have to kind of chuckle now when I am asked about it because I almost forget that it is even there. I could either fret over it or think of it as a unique gift from my Creator. I am at a point in my life where I see it as the latter, and I even like it because it is something that makes me special, and it was given to me by God.

However, the second insecurity, the one I feel I will struggle with for the rest of my life, is my body's unique ability to awkwardly blush almost instantaneously for no real reason at all. It isn't just a case of rosy cheeks, believe me; that would not bother me at all! My body blushes in a way that looks like I have just broken out into a severe case of hives, and I have absolutely no control over it at all. In fact, the more I concern myself with it, the worse it becomes. I remember begging my mother to let me wear makeup as an early teen because I was mortified anytime this happened—not that makeup really helped a whole lot, but it was kind of like a security blanket. My mind somehow imagined that it masked some of the evidence.

You can imagine the countless awkward moments this insecurity has created, not to mention the ocean of tears I have wept over this lifelong obstacle. I almost feel as if this insecurity has somewhat squelched the personality that hides within my soul. I have creatively come up with ways to avoid specific situations like being the center of attention, speaking in front of people, or being in a location where I could easily get overheated. I even feel that this insecurity may have, in a way, cost me my heart's deepest desire. I guess I will never know that for sure until I get to heaven, but the one thing I do know is that I must continually run to the scriptures. I know, through scripture, that God has created me and that He knew all about this insecurity before I was even created. He knew this would be a struggle for me, and He knew this would draw me closer to Him.

# Overcoming Any Insecurity

Believe me, I have had numerous moments in my life where I have fallen into Satan's trap and allowed myself to believe the lies that he has to offer. I have allowed myself to feel self-pity, anger, resentment, and more. Elisabeth Elliot warns of the awful feeling of self-pitty. She says, "Refuse self-pity. Refuse it absolutely. It is a deadly thing with the power to destroy you. Turn your thoughts to Christ who has already carried our griefs and sorrows."

But when I go back to the Word, to the precious promises of my Lord and Savior, I again obtain the peace that He alone can give. "And the peace of God, which passeth all understanding, shall keep your hearts and minds through Christ Jesus" (Philippians 4:7).

I chose the scripture that I refer to as my "life verse" because it reminds me always to trust God, even when I do not understand; to live for Him, and He will lead me, guide me, and direct me in all paths of my life. It says, "Trust in the Lord with all thine heart; and lean not unto thine own understanding. In all thy ways acknowledge him, and he shall direct thy paths" (Proverbs 3:5–6).

I have learned that this insecurity can either rule my life, or I can allow Christ to work through it for my good and for His glory. I must put it completely in His hands. Perhaps it is also a way of Him keeping me humble. There is very rarely a day that goes by when I do not pray about this insecurity in some capacity. No matter how life-altering an insecurity can sometimes seem, God can take that insecurity and use it to honor and glorify Himself, if we allow Him to do so. In fact, if I had never experienced these things for myself, I would not be able to relate to others who also struggle with insecurities, and I could not help them overcome those. I would like to share with you three things that I have found to be tried-and-true helps in these oppressive times of my own life's journey:

- First, go to the scriptures. Find a passage, a precious promise, and keep it close to you. Read it often and put it to memory. Quote it, claim it, cling to it, and God will deliver you from the oppression. "Thy word have I hid in mine heart, that I might not sin against thee" (Psalm 119:11).
- Second, go to the Lord in prayer. I remember a quote I once saw that said, "Have you prayed about it as much as you have talked about it?" Who do you discuss these issues with? Take it to the Lord! He can deliver you and perform great and mighty works in your life. "Call unto me, and I will answer thee, and shew thee great and mighty things, which thou knowest not" (Jeremiah 33:3).
- Third, seek godly counsel. If you have claimed scripture and have talked to God about the issue, but you feel that you need to speak to someone about it, seek godly counsel. That could be your pastor, your pastor's wife, or an older, more mature Christian in your life. God puts specific people in our lives for a reason. "A wise man will hear, and will increase learning;

and a man of understanding shall attain unto wise counsels" (Proverbs 1:5).

Always remember, if it is in God's Word, it is true! When God says you are loved, Believe Him! When He says you are precious, Believe Him!

# Believe Him

by Lee Black, Joel Linsey, and Sue C. Smith

I know you believe He's our Maker,
Creator of Heaven and Earth.
You've never doubted His miracles
Or the wonder surrounding His birth.
So why would you listen to even a whisper,
Stealing your joy somehow?
May I just remind you, He's already spoken.
Oh, can't you hear Him now?
If God says your loved, Believe Him!
When He says your precious, Believe Him!
You can trust that He cares for you;
Knows what you're going through.
He feels every burden you bear.
He'll be there whenever you need Him, Believe Him!
He spoke it the loudest on Calvary.
He said with the Cross you are mine.
He wrote it in red for the world to see,
And He settled it there for all time!
So why would you listen, to even a whisper,
Steeling your joy somehow?
May I just remind you, He's already spoken.
Won't you Believe Him now?
If God says your loved, Believe Him!
When He says you're precious, Believe Him!
You can trust that He cares for you,
Knows what you're going through.
He feels every burden you bear.
He'll be there whenever you need Him, Believe Him!
You can have faith in each promise.
In His Word He has told you Himself.

Believe that He's Holy and Mighty and Just;
But friend more than anything else,
If God says your loved, Believe Him!
When He says you're precious, Believe Him!
You can trust that He cares for you,
Knows what you're going through.
He feels every burden you bear.
He'll be there whenever you need Him, Believe Him!
Believe Him! You can Believe Him![2]

*My Hope*

*is Found in*

*Christ Alone*

# God Is My Sustainer

To sustain means to strengthen or support physically or mentally. Through creation, God has given us everything required to physically sustain humankind. He has given us rain to grow food, plants to feed animals, a mind to know how to grow, harvest, and cook food, and to survive. God has also given humanity the necessary intelligence to invent and develop a plethora of resources to sustain us physically—and quite comfortably, might I add. God has also made ways to sustain us mentally. He created a system by which we tell time: the sun to rule the day and the moon to rule the night, a variety of seasons with all their different temperatures, weather patterns, and more.

God also gives us what we need to sustain us spiritually. Through His shed blood, He has given us hope for eternity. Have you ever felt hopeless? Hopelessness is not a very pleasant feeling, yet countless numbers of people, Christians included, live in a hopeless state daily. You may say, "How could a Christian feel hopeless? If they have truly accepted Christ as their Savior, their eternity is sealed." That is true; you cannot lose your salvation. God's Word says, "And I give unto them eternal life; and they shall never perish, neither shall any man pluck them out of my hand" (John 10:28).

However, have you ever experienced a situation or circumstance in your life when you just really had a hard time trusting God? If we can trust God for our eternal destinies, we should be able to trust God through every situation, no matter how big or how small, in our daily lives. Charles Spurgeon once said, "To trust God in the light is nothing but trust him in the dark—that is Faith."

# My Own Personal Experience
# of Feeling Hopeless

Again, I find myself going to the truths found in my "life verse": "Trust in the Lord with all thine heart; and lean not unto thine own understanding. In all thy ways acknowledge him, and he shall direct thy paths" (Proverbs 3:5–6).

I am going to make myself completely vulnerable for just a moment and share with you a situation in my own life that I have a really hard time completely trusting God with—and, in fact, at times, I feel just that, hopeless..

Everyone has somewhat of a stereotypical "vision" of how their lives should play out. I had, from a very young age, envisioned myself graduating from high school, going to college, and, while in college, finding that "perfect man" whom I always knew God had in His plan for my life. However, I graduated from college, and that "vision" did not play out. I then went on to work at the school I graduated from for about seven years and conveniently changed my vision to the idea that God's plan was for me to meet my future husband in this season of my life. Well, those seven years past, and again, this vision of my life still did not play out the way I had hoped. I then proceeded to move back home, thinking maybe "he" was there all the time. To make a long story short, still to this day, my vision of what I thought my life should be like has not played out the way I had always hoped. In fact, the prime of my life has quickly fleeted from me, and there are times that I feel I have wasted this portion of my life pining after something that God obviously did not have in His perfect plan for my life. This has been a hard pill to swallow and very difficult to accept—and has left me at times feeling quite hopeless. According to Rachel Marie Martin, "Sometimes you have to let go of the picture of what you thought life would be like and learn to find joy in the story you are actually living."

I want you to know that my situation can be replaced with any situation that you may be experiencing. For me, this is very near and dear to my heart, and therefore, to me, it has been absolutely devastating because it has always been my heart's deepest desire to get married and have a family. Some may not empathize with me because they do not quite understand the deepness of this desire. I just ask that you replace my desire with a desire from your own life. Has something tragic happened and left you dependent on someone or something that you have deeply desired God to change, but He has not allowed it to? On the other hand, I may not empathize with you because I may not completely understand your situation. I just want you to know that God can work in similar ways for drastically different or opposite situations.

Rachel Marie Martin says, "The ugly part of your story that you are living through right now is going to be one of the most powerful parts of your testimony." My passion is either to help you personally or to encourage you to help someone else who is going through what seems like such a tragedy in their own hearts. Elisabeth Elliot said, "When [our plans] are interrupted, His are not. His plans are proceeding exactly as scheduled, moving us always (including those minutes or hours or years which seem most useless or wasted or unendurable)."

I was given the following verse by a very godly woman whom I have always looked up to and sought godly counsel from, and I will always be grateful to her for pointing me to the Bible for comfort and direction. "Delight thyself also in the Lord: and he shall give thee the desires of thine heart" (Psalm 37:4).

The word *delight* means to please greatly. I mentioned before that, at times, I feel I have wasted the prime of my life. Although I have indeed wasted specific portions of my life—those times being when I have allowed myself to be discouraged and downtrodden—I cannot say that I have wasted all of this time, because I have continuously sought to "delight" myself in the Lord wherever He has led me—even when my heart just ached with desperation. This personal desire, although currently unfulfilled, remains my heart's deepest longing. I have found myself struggling to trust God with that part of my life because I have felt, at times, that I have complete faith that He could bring a man into my life, but for whatever reason, He has chosen to deny me this desire. Elisabeth Elliot once said, "The life of faith is lived one day at a time, and it has to be lived—not always looked forward to as though the 'real' living were around the next corner."

There are days that I just beg God to remove this desire if it is not a part of His perfect plan, but even though I have had feelings of hopelessness, I choose to trust Him because God is in complete control, knows all things, and wants only what is best for me, even though I do not understand. A quote by Mandy Hale says, "God, help me to see the good in the 'not knowing', the joy in the 'in-between', the meaning in the 'meantime.'"

# Overcoming Hopelessness

Amid all the turmoil of these ups and downs of life, I am reminded of the following verses and inspirational quotes from Christians who have "been there": "Wait on the Lord: be of good courage, and he shall strengthen thine heart: wait, I say, on the Lord" (Psalm 27:14).

Be encouraged. God has not forgotten about you. He loves you and wants only what is best for you. I agree with Elizabeth Elliot's quote, "Peace does in outward things, but in the heart prepared to wait trustfully and quietly on Him who has all things safely in His hands."

It is in these times that He strengthens your heart and shows Himself mighty. "I wait for the Lord, my soul doth wait, and in his word do I hope" (Psalm 130:5). All the hope you will ever need is found in God's Word.

"Continue in prayer, and watch in the same with thanksgiving" (Colossians 4:2). Whatever your situation, take it to the Lord in prayer and thank Him for the paths that He brings you through. You never know how He will use these circumstances or what He is preparing you for through these difficult times.

Elisabeth Elliot once said, "Prayer lays hold of God's plan and becomes the link between His will and its accomplishment on earth.

Amazing things happen, and we are given the privilege of being the channels of the Holy Spirit's prayer."

Most of the unforeseen paths in life are meant to prepare us for something that we may not even be aware of at that time. "Commit thy way unto the Lord, trust also in Him and He shall bring it to pass" (Psalm 37:5). Trust God. Live for Him. Do not stray from Him. Trust in His timing, and you will always be pleased with how He brings things to pass. As Nancy Leigh DeMoss explains, "In every season, in every circumstance, His Grace is sufficient for me."

There is always hope in Jesus! "And let us not be weary in well doing: for in due season we shall reap, if we faint not." (Galatians 6:9). Still, waiting is not an easy journey. But I have found that there is still hope in waiting.

According to Elisabeth Elliot, "God is God. Because He is God. He is worthy of my trust and obedience. I will find rest nowhere but in His holy will that is unspeakable beyond my largest notions of what He is up to."

I do not want God's second best. I do not want my best; I want exactly who God has chosen as perfect for me. Is it easy to wait? Absolutely not. But amid this trial, again I find myself drawing closer to my Savior. "And therefore will the Lord wait, that he may be gracious unto you, and therefore will he be exalted, that he may have mercy upon you: for the Lord is a God of judgment: blessed are all they that wait for him" (Isaiah 30:18).

My desire is for God to be exalted in my life and for others to see Him through me. According to Elisabeth Elliot, "God never withholds from His child that which His love and wisdom call good. God's refusals are always merciful—'severe mercies' at times, but mercies all the same. God never denies us our heart's desire except to give us something better."

There is a song that I often listen to, entitled, "For My Good and for His Glory." He works all things for our good that He may be glorified amid our struggles. "And we know that all things work together for good to them that love God, to them who are the called according to his purpose" (Romans 8:28).

I know that God has a purpose in this season of waiting, no matter how long that wait may be. I have chosen to trust my Savior, my Creator, my sustainer. He has never failed me, and I know He is at work. I also must remind myself that the things we wait for the longest are often the sweetest and less taken for granted. "For my thoughts are not your thoughts, neither are your ways my ways, saith the Lord. For as the heavens are higher than the earth, so are my ways higher than your ways, and my thoughts than your thoughts" (Isaiah 55:8–9).

He knows the big picture. Keep your eyes on Him. He knows how everything will play out, and He has your best at interest. Psalms 32:8 says, "I will instruct thee and teach thee in the way which thou shalt go: I will guide thee with mine eye." And 1 Corinthians 2:9 says, "But as it is written, Eye hath not seen, nor ear heard, neither have entered into the heart of man, the things which God hath prepared for them that love him."

He loves you. Trust Him! God bottles each and every tear that we cry, and He knows every heartache that we have ever or will ever go through. Trust Him!

This online quote found on Pinterest by @princessfavour_1 is very encouraging to me. It says, "And when you are staring into the eyes of your answered prayer, the pain will fade, and joy will be your new song. Restoration will be your portion *and only God will get the glory*" (emphasis added).

Serve God and grow as a Christian in the meantime. Don't put your life on hold while you are in the season of waiting. Take it as an opportunity to keep busy serving the Lord and learning more about

Him. This may even be a time of preparation that God is allowing so that when that time of waiting is over, you will be ready for the next step in His perfect plan.

Denise J. Hughes once said, "God has designed every detail of our lives with intention and purpose." We do not always understand, but that is okay. If we can trust God for our whole of eternity, we can trust Him for this vapor that we refer to as life. "Whereas ye know not what shall be on the morrow. For what is your life? It is even a vapour, that appeareth for a little time, and then vanisheth away" (James 4:14).

Take things one day at a time, and continuously seek the Lord for guidance and direction. Know that God's plan is perfect. Don't make the mistake of narrowing down your vision to what the "norm" is or what you think is expected. Allow God to broaden your horizons and use you to your fullest potential. It is during this time that you may find some hidden gems that would otherwise never have been revealed. "And not only so, but we glory in tribulations also: knowing that tribulation worketh patience; And patience, experience; and experience, hope" (Romans 5:3–4).

Let Him refine you and mold you. There is a phrase in a song that I think of often, and it says, "You planned your perfect purpose for me on this earth." What powerful words, and what a wonderful thought that God has a specific purpose for you on this earth. Trust Him! "He that dwelleth in the secret place of the most High shall abide under the shadow of the Almighty. I will say of the Lord, He is my refuge and my fortress: my God; in Him will I trust" (Psalms 91:1–2).

Completely surrender your life to Him. Even when we do not understand, we can fully trust Him! Let Him write your story. It will be a whole lot better than any story we could come up with on our own!

# Lord, Here's My Life

by Mikayla Murray-Gonzalez

I knew exactly how I wanted my own life to go,
No heartaches, No failures,
No disappointments to unfold.
But, God had a different plan
For what life would bring my way.
And although I may not understand,
I can trust the Lord and say:
"Here's my Life; I surrender
All my plans and all my dreams
That I thought were best for me.
Use my life for Your glory.
Take the pen from my hand, and write out Your story."
And although I may never fully understand,
I want to be willing to say,
"Lord, here's my life."
You may be struggling with trials of your own.
You cannot see God's plan for you;
You feel so all alone.
Oh, but God's way is perfect.
He guides each step you take.
And although it's hard to see it now,
You can trust the Lord and say:
"Here's my life; I surrender
All my plans and all my dreams
That I thought were best for me.
Use my life for Your glory.
Take the pen from my hand,
And write out Your story."
And although I may never fully understand,
I want to be willing to say:

"Take my life, and let it be
Consecrated, Lord, to Thee."
"Here's my life; I surrender
All my plans and all my dreams
That I thought were best for me.
Use my life for Your glory.
Take the pen from my hand, and write out Your story."
And although I may never fully understand,
I want to be willing to say:
"Lord, here's my life."[3]

---

[3] "Lord, Here's My Life," by Mikayla Murray-Gonzalez, ©2018. All rights reserved; used with permission.

There's No

Other Friend

Like Jesus

# God Is My Friend and My Comforter

I combine these two topics because I believe they go hand in hand.

We often seek comfort from a close friend or perhaps from a parent. Is God your friend? A friend is someone whom you know and have a bond of mutual liking. The longer you walk with God and grow spiritually, the greater the bond grows between you and your Savior. He becomes a true friend whom you can go to with absolutely anything and everything. "A man that hath friends must shew himself friendly: and there is a friend that sticketh closer than a brother" (Proverbs 18:24).

I have been blessed with many friends throughout the course of my life, and I am truly grateful to God for each of them. God has a purpose for everyone who crosses our paths. Whether they are sent from God to be a help to you, or God has sent them for you to be a help to them, no one ever crosses our paths by accident. "Ointment and perfume rejoice the heart; so doth the sweetness of a man's friend by hearty counsel" (Proverbs 27:9).

Some friends are family, some are church friends, some are college friends, some are childhood friends, some are lifelong, and some are just sent to you for a short time. Whoever they are, I have found that friends come and go; friendships grow and fade away; circumstances can produce distance between friendships; but the one friend whom I can always count on to be there for me is God. Did you know that you can go to Him at any time, season, or from any distance in your life? You choose your distance from God. He is always there; it is we who may stray away from time to time. "Draw nigh to God, and he will draw nigh to you" (James 4:8a).

Have you ever experienced loneliness? I have. Loneliness is an unusual feeling. There have been times that I have found myself surrounded by people (family, friends, coworkers), yet I still felt a deep loneliness. Perhaps your circumstances seem isolated, and you feel that no one else will understand your unique position. When you are feeling lonely, it may be that you have strayed away from God, or it may be that you just long for a specific type of human relationship. God designed us to need human companionship.

As a single person, many times I have found myself longing for a spouse to share a story or a special experience with. Some things are just meant to be shared within a specific relationship. Maybe you have lost a spouse or loved one and you feel a loneliness because that person is no longer here with you. When we are overcome by the feeling of loneliness, we often seek comfort.

As I have mentioned before, it should be our goal to get to the point where we allow God to be our everything. Not only is He a friend, but He is a friend who can comfort like no other. "Blessed be God, even the Father of our Lord Jesus Christ, the Father of mercies, and the God of all comfort; Who comforteth us in all our tribulation, that we may be able to comfort them which are in any trouble, by the comfort wherewith we ourselves are comforted of God" (2 Corinthians 1:3–4).

God offers a comfort that can sooth the soul, but you must accept it. Sometimes we tend to be overcome by loneliness, and we just do not want to accept the comfort that God offers. Don't waste precious time letting Satan consume you with these feelings when God is waiting to give you a comfort that is indescribable. I have often found great comfort in going to the Comforter, the one who hears and understands when I do not even have the words to express the pain. He understands even the tears of a broken heart. "The Lord is nigh unto them that are of a broken heart; and saveth such as be of a contrite spirit. Many are the afflictions of the righteous: but the Lord delivereth him out of them all" (Psalm 34:18–19).

# My Own Personal Experience
# of Loneliness

Again, I speak of my own experience because that is what I know, but think of how my experience can relate in your personal situation. Perhaps you have lost a precious child, a beloved spouse, or even a close friend. These circumstances can often leave us feeling lonely because we do not have, or no longer have, those relationships that we so desire. Just remember that God can comfort the lonely heart. He can fill that void, and He knows and understands even when it seems you are all alone.

I may be a little silly to feel sorrow over these things, but there are times that tears just stream down my cheeks as I wonder if there will ever be a day when I get to experience these moments for myself. I often contemplate whether I will ever experience being the bride. I have been honored to be in numerous weddings as a bridesmaid, but I still long for the day that I am walking down the aisle in a white gown adorned for my beloved. It has pretty much become an ongoing joke with me because I have frequently caught the bride's bouquet during the bouquet toss. I tell people that the bouquets do not work for me because I have caught so many, yet I remain single. In this area, I often must fight off my own selfish feelings, and I must purposefully decide to choose joy even amid sorrow. I love weddings in general and am thrilled for the new couple that joins together in holy matrimony, but many times, I still feel a sorrow in my own heart, a loneliness, because I, too, desire to have someone to share my life with while on this earth. I do not want just to experience the wedding day, but also falling in love, receiving flowers "just because," or even the feeling of being loved or wanted.

There is a specific loneliness when surrounded by women who are all married and have children. Yes, we are all women, and we are alike in that way, but there is a specific loneliness that is felt, almost like you have no "category." You are not a wife; you are not a mother. You are just … there. I enjoy seeing the interactions between a mother and a child, but sometimes it hurts because it makes me wonder if I will ever experience having a child of my own. I have had women say to me, "I am so jealous; you have so much time to do what you want. You want to trade places?" It breaks my heart because, yes, I would trade places. As a single person, your position typically falls into the babysitter category. Don't get me wrong; I love children, but it sometimes brings a sorrow that is not always visible, but deeply felt.

Sometimes a holiday will roll around, and my heart gets heavy. On Mother's Day, I love to honor and celebrate my own mother, but I can't help to think that I may not ever have a child to wish me happy Mother's Day. I may not ever have the opportunity to be called *mom*. I may not ever experience motherhood, and it just weighs heavy on my heart. I also think of the future, and the loneliness of having no grandchildren to enjoy. I know that God has promised always to be with me and to take care of me, but when I am old, what will life be like with no children or grandchildren to love and cherish? I must leave my unknown future to a known God whom I know is in control and who will not leave me fruitless.

# Overcoming Loneliness

The very first thing to do for overcoming these feelings of loneliness is not to dwell on what you do not have, but rather remember how good God has been and what He has blessed you with. We must always remain thankful, not just in the easy parts of life but also in the hard parts of life. We must always give thanks to God. As I always like to say, "There is a reason for everything." The scripture in 1 Thessalonians 5:18 says, "In every thing give thanks: for this is the will of God in Christ Jesus concerning you."

This is the very reason that I cut my own experience short in this chapter. I do not like to talk about these things; neither do I think God wants me to dwell on them. You must not let loneliness steal your joy. You can have joy even amid sorrow, and though your feelings are very real, they do not have to dominate your outlook on life or your attitude. "But rejoice, inasmuch as ye are partakers of Christ's sufferings; that, when His glory shall be revealed, ye may be glad also with exceeding joy" (1 Peter 4:13).

The last thing I want is for people to feel sorry for me or to pity me. I do, however, feel it is important to think of others' feelings. One of the greatest life lessons I have ever learned is to put myself in someone else's shoes, which is also a biblical concept. "Therefore all things whatsoever ye would that men should do to you, do ye even so to them: for this is the law and the prophets" (Matthew 7:12).

How would I feel if I was the person in a low place in life and struggling to stay afloat? How would I feel if I was the mother who had a sick child and felt helpless and afraid? How would I feel if I was the punch line of a seemingly "harmless" joke that just wasn't necessary? Putting yourself in someone else's place will also help you think before you act. The younger you are when learning this lesson, the better. It will give you a better perspective on what others are going through and how you can be a help and an encouragement to them.

Jesus Himself would be the greatest example of "putting yourself in someone else's shoes." He literally put Himself in the shoes of all humanity. He took on our sins, suffered, bled, and died to make a way for the unworthy. What a selfless act of pure love. So, when you feel that you have been forgotten or just feel alone, turn to the one who is always there, even in the darkest hours of your life. Joy is a choice. It is a conscious decision you must make, sometimes daily. No matter what storm or valley I may be going through, I still choose to believe. Because God is my friend and my greatest comfort.

# I Still Believe

## by Adri Ludwick

Darkness came and brought a storm
My world was torn apart.
With broken heart and tear stained eyes
I stumbled in the dark.
But you were there for every step,
Your hand was guiding me.
So through my tears, the pain and grief
I choose to Still Believe!
I still believe your way is right.
I still trust in Your plan.
I still believe in miracles,
Though I don't understand.
I still believe you know what's best,
I'll follow where you lead.
So with all the pieces of my broken heart
I Still Believe!
Prince of Peace, the Comforter
On you I can depend.
Your God Almighty, King of All,
Yet you choose to be my friend.
Your grace is all-sufficient,
And Your strength is all I need.
So through this storm I'll praise your name
and choose to Still Believe!
I still believe your way is right.
I still trust in your plan.
I still believe in miracles,
Though I don't understand.
I still believe you know what's best.
I'll follow where you lead.

So with all the pieces of my broken heart
I Still Believe!
I still trust in your plan.
I still believe in miracles,
Though I don't understand.
I still believe you know what's best.
I'll follow where you lead.
So, with all the pieces of my broken heart, I Still Believe![4]

---

[4] "I Still Believe" by Adri Ludwick. Music Faculty Hyles-Anderson College, ©2016 Adri Ludwick Music. All rights reserved; used with permission.

*God's Been*
*Good in*
*My Life*

# God Is Good and Only Good

Did you know that God is good and only good? Did you? This is a truth! He is *good* and can only ever be *good*. Do you believe that, with your whole heart? The book of Psalms is an excellent place to go to find many of the gold nuggets of God's goodness. Here are a few examples:

- "For the Lord is *good*; his mercy is everlasting; and his truth endureth to all generations" (Psalms 100:5).
- "O taste and see that the Lord is *good*: blessed is the man that trusteth in him" (Psalm 34:8).
- "Praise the Lord; for the Lord is *good*: sing praises unto his name; for it is pleasant." (Psalm 135:3).
- "The Lord is *good* to all: and his tender mercies are over all his works." (Psalm 145:9).

Although this is a truth that I know, I have, at times, allowed the circumstances of my life to overshadow this truth. I love how Christine Caine says it, "All the disappointment in the world will never change the promises of God."

Sometimes we as Christians allow doubt to creep into our lives. Though we know that God is good, there are times we may doubt His goodness. Doubt is a feeling of uncertainty or a lack of conviction. Many times, this doubt comes through circumstances that leave you feeling as if God has left you or doesn't love you. I know of many people, myself included, who have gauged God's goodness upon the current circumstances in our lives. God is good because He says that He is good. His character allows Him only to be good. When unforeseen circumstances come into our lives, they are not a test of God's goodness but rather, in many instances, a test of our faith.

Take the story of Job, for instance. If we gauged the goodness of God upon the circumstances that Job went through, we would have to conclude that God is not always good. Yes, God allowed those things to happen to Job, but not because He was not being good to him. God knew that His servant Job would remain faithful even amid the most devastating of circumstances. Many times, it is during these trying times of our lives that God is growing our faith. He is molding us, sometimes under great pressure. He is refining us, sometimes under great heat. This is part of the growing process. If we were never put under pressure or heat, we would never become the intricately designed vessels or the beautifully polished diamonds that God is turning us into for His glory.

# My Own Experience of Doubting God's Goodness

I have truly been blessed in my lifetime. I know of many people who have gone through some of the toughest circumstances, and I am so grateful for God's grace in my life. I do recall a time in my life, however, when I felt like my world was crashing all around me. I was on the brink of becoming a teenager (the hormones were raging), my family was moving to a different town and a different house, we were amid a nasty church split and were looking for a new church to attend, and I was having to do some things on my own for the first time and was simply terrified. However, it was during this time in my life that God was working in my heart about my salvation. I often wonder if the things in my life would have remained the way they were and if life would not have become "rocky" if I would have ever come to the place where I admitted I was lost and truly asked Christ to save me. I am so thankful for God's goodness in that seemingly bad time in my life. God allowed those things to happen for a reason, and I am so thankful for His goodness in that area.

In more recent years, it has been hard not to doubt God's goodness because my life has played out drastically different than how I always thought it would. I thought that by the time I turned forty, I would be happily married with seven children, and probably some of those children would already be grown and going off on their own. Never in a million years did I see myself as still being single, but through it all, God has been faithful, and He has been so good.

# Choosing to Believe God's Goodness

Despite how certain circumstances have played out in my own life, I do not want to become bitter. I want to always be kind, and I can't help but think that one must be somewhat courageous to attempt to go through life by faith, leaning on God's goodness to get through every unknown next step. Elisabeth Elliot puts it this way, "Waiting on God requires the willingness to bear uncertainty, to carry within oneself the unanswered question, lifting the heart to God about it whenever it intrudes upon one's thoughts."

I have, on many occasions, had to take my doubts to God and, by faith, trust that He knows my future and that He will safely carry me in the palm of His capable hands through my most uncertain times. I cannot in any way doubt God's goodness toward me, because despite not getting or having what I wanted in life, He has always taken very good care of me.

I may not understand. I may not know why. I may not know when or how or if, but I do know He has promised that if I delight in Him, He will give me the desires of my heart. Sometimes this makes me ask the question—is this truly my heart's desire? Above all, I desire to fulfill the purpose that God put me on this earth to accomplish through Him.

Is that purpose what I want or just what I thought I wanted? I have a series of questions I have recently asked myself when I am trying to determine what God's desire is for my life:

1. Would I allow this desire to surpass my Savior? Would this desire become a "god" to me? He will never give you something that will draw you away from Himself.
2. Does He have a greater purpose for me? Many times, this causes thoughts of resentment. Perhaps someone needs me, and if He fulfilled my heart's desire, then I might not serve in the capacity that He has equipped me for.

Elisabeth Elliot once said, "Sometimes we want things we were not meant to have. Because he loves us, the Father says no. Faith trusts that no. Faith is willing not to have what God is not willing to give. Furthermore, faith does not insist upon an explanation. It is enough to know His promises to give what is good—He knows so much more about us than we do."

# He Is Enough

by Mikayla Murray-Gonzalez

When we feel the world is crashing all around us,
We're helpless and afraid;
God seems so far away.
Oh, but He's a faithful Friend.
He is with us 'til the end.
So don't you fear
For God is ever near.
He is enough; (He's enough)
Jesus meets my needs.
He satisfies my longing heart;
He's been so good to me.
He is enough
In a dry and thirsty land,
In the midst of the valley
When I can't trace the Father's hand.
And when my strength fails, and I feel I can't go on;
Jesus reminds me of His love.
He is enough.
Are you walking through
Some heartache and pain?
You don't understand how it's all in the Father's plan.
Oh, but, Friend, let me tell you,
He sees your ev'ry tear.
In your weakest moments,
He will always be near.
He is enough; (He's enough)
Jesus meets my needs.
He satisfies my longing heart;
He's been so good to me.
He is Enough

In a dry and thirsty land,
In the midst of the valley
When I can't trace the Father's hand.
And when my strength fails, and I feel I can't go on;
Jesus reminds me of His Love.
He is Enough.
Oh, and when you can't go on,
He will be Enough.
When your strength is almost gone,
He will be Enough.
When the pathway grows dim,
Place your trust in Him.
When the road ahead gets tough,
He will be Enough!
He is Enough; (He's enough)
Jesus meets my needs.
He satisfies my longing heart;
He's been so good to me.
He is Enough
In a dry and thirsty land,
In the midst of the valley
When I can't trace the Father's hand.
And when my strength fails,
And I feel I can't go on;
Jesus reminds me of His love.
He is Enough.[5]

---

3. Is His "no" an unknown mercy in my life? Is this a matter of something greater than even my own comprehension? Does He have a greater "yes" coming instead?

According to Elisabeth Elliot, "He says no in order that He may, in some way we cannot imagine, say yes. All his ways with us are merciful. His meaning is always love."

4. Is my desire ultimately not His desire? Has my desire, although not against His Word, not been His desire for me?

# Not My Will

by Chloe Van Dyke-Harris

When He was in the garden
In His darkest hour of life,
Jesus prayed to His Father
With anguish deep inside.
He didn't want to suffer,
But greater was His love.
He surrendered to God's will
And raised His eyes above.
Not my Will; (not my will)
I lay it at Your feet.
Not my will; (not my will)
I find a peace so sweet
In yielding my ambitions,
My hopes, and all my dreams.
You always work more good
Than I could ever scheme;
So not my will, (not my will)
But Thine be done.
Sometimes you close the door,
And the next one opens up.
Sometimes we're left in the hallway,
And the waiting feels unjust.
Then you show me all the people
That are passing by.
While I wait for Your direction,
Your name I'll magnify!
Not my will; (not my will)
I lay it at your feet.
Not my will; (not my will)
I find a peace so sweet

In yielding my ambitions,
My hopes, and all my dreams.
You always work more good
Than I could ever scheme;
So not my will; (not my will)
But Thine be done.
My life, Lord, is Yours to control,
I give You my heart and my soul.
I'll seek Your will, never mine,
Rich treasures to find.
Not my will; (not my will)
I lay it at your feet.
Not my will; (not my will)
I find a peace so sweet
In yielding my ambitions
My hopes, and all my dreams.
You always work more good
Than I could ever scheme;
So not my will; (not my will)
But Thine be done.
My life, Lord, is yours to control.[6]

[6] "Not My Will" by Chloe Van Dyke-Harris, ©2019. All rights reserved; used with permission.

5. God may still fulfill this desire one day, but is He allowing me to go through this trying time of waiting to refine me, to prove me, or to prepare me?

I have always wanted only God's perfect will for my life, and although at times I am overcome with the grief of realizing that my desire may never be fulfilled, my greatest desire is to please my Lord and to live for Him. He loves me, He died for me, He saved me, He created me, He sustains me, He knows me better than I know myself, and He has never lied to me. I am left with the only thing I know to lean on, and that is the promises of His Word. Is He good? Yes! He is because His Word says that He is, and I choose to put my trust in Him. As Elisabeth Elliot says, "The only thing that keeps me stable and settled in these days of uncertainty is the absolute dependability of God's Word."

# You Are Always Good

**by Chris Anderson**
**music by Jonathan Hamilton**

Looking back, I can see Your fingerprints upon my life
Always seeking my best.
There were times when Your way would make no sense;
But as You said, You have never left.
You are always good; You are only good.
You are always good to me.
Though my eyes can't see,
Help my heart believe
You are always only good.
Looking in, I can see my frailty;
My sin is great,
And my strength is so small.
Still You stay, and Your mercy shelters me;
You hold my hand, and You hear my call.
You are always good; You are only good.
You are always good to me.
Though my eyes can't see,
Help my heart believe
You are always only good.
Looking up, I can see Your sympathy;
I doubt myself, but I'm sure of Your Love.
Lavish grace was poured out at Calvary,
Securing me for our home above.
You are always good; You are only good.

You are always good to me.
Though my eyes can't see,
Help my heart believe
You are always, only good.[7]

[7] "You Are Always Good," words by Chris Anderson, music by Jonathan Hamilton, ©2014 by Majesty Music, Inc. All rights reserved; used by permission.

Walk with
Him and
Talk with
Him

# God Is My Provider

Let's face it, we all have needs. Some needs are greater than others, but we all have them. Did you know that God has promised to provide for *all* our needs? "But my God shall supply all your need according to his riches in glory by Christ Jesus" (Philippians 4:19).

Now, you'll notice that this verse says, "all your needs," not "all your wants." If you have a legitimate need, then you can rest assured that God will supply that. The verse also says, "according to his riches." I've heard it said something like this: "My God owns all the cattle on all the hills, and all the taters too!" Psalms 50:10 says, "For every beast of the forest is mine, and the cattle upon a thousand hills."

Don't you think that God, who spoke the world into existence and planned for you to inhabit this earth for such a time as this, would provide the things you need to fulfil the plan that He has made specifically for you? We also know that He does not supply only our needs, but it also pleases Him to give us many of our wants and desires as well. "If ye then, being evil, know how to give good gifts unto your children, how much more shall your Father which is in heaven give good things to them that ask him?" (Matthew 7:11).

Just like a parent would desire to lavish his or her children with earthly goods, God, even more so, desires to give us good things. You will notice though, the verse says, "to them that ask Him." How many times have I thought, *Man I wish I could afford that* or *Wouldn't that be nice if I could go there*? Then I must ask myself, have I asked God for it? "Ask, and it shall be given you; seek, and ye shall find; knock, and it shall be opened unto you: For every one that asketh receiveth; and he that seeketh findeth; and to him that knocketh it shall be opened" (Matthew 7:7–8).

Prayer is one of the most important aspects of a Christian's spiritual walk with God. When we pray, we are talking to God, the one who has promised to supply all our needs and the one who has said, "Ask, and it shall be given you." How is your prayer life? If I am completely honest, I will have to say that my prayer life has not always been consistent. There have been times in my walk with God when I have been lazy. He gives us *power* in prayer, and yet sometimes we don't utilize that power simply because we are lazy. Go to God! Talk to God! Build your relationship with your Savior! You will never regret the fruit that comes from a healthy prayer life.

# My Own Experience of Growing a Fruitful Prayer Life

$A$s I have mentioned previously, I was saved at a young age. I did pray about things, but it was not until college, when I heard a message about prayer, that prayer really came *alive* to me! Does it take time? Yes! Does it have to be planned? Yes! Is it worth it? Absolutely! Many Christians go through their lives half-heartedly praying about things, not believing that God will answer their prayers. Do you know how many marvelous promises are in the Bible about prayer? Many, many, many wonderful promises!

There are several verses that I claim often. This is a verse that my mom and I claim when we are praying about something together. I have seen God answer many prayers when we have claimed this verse together and have watched God work: "Again I say unto you, That if two of you shall agree on earth as touching any thing that they shall ask, it shall be done for them of my Father which is in heaven" (Matthew 18:19).

Do we give praise to God when He answers specific prayers? We should! Shout it from the rooftops; proclaim it from the mountaintops!

"And whatsoever ye shall ask in my name, that will I do, that the Father may be glorified in the Son" (John 14:13).

The scriptures in 1 John 5:14–15 say, "And this is the confidence that we have in him, if we ask any thing according to his will, he heareth us: And if we know that he hear us, whatsoever we ask, we know we have the petitions that we desired of him."

II Peter 3:9 is the verse I claim many times when I am praying for someone's salvation. It is always God's will for people to be saved. I have family members for whose salvation I have prayed for many, many years. I still pray, believing that He will save them! "The Lord is not slack concerning his promise, as some men count slackness; but is longsuffering to us-ward, not willing that any should perish, but that all should come to repentance" (2 Peter 3:9).

Prayer, believing that God will do something, is also very important. Do you truly believe that God can and will do what we ask? "And all things, whatsoever ye shall ask in prayer, believing, ye shall receive" (Matthew 21:22).

I specifically remember the semester in college when I began to see a fruitful prayer life. I prayed, believing that God would do specific things, and watched as God answered prayer after prayer. I remember having some things on my prayer list that would have been considered impossible by human standards. Those are the best kind of prayer requests! Pray for something impossible and see God answer in miraculous ways. Luke 1:37 says, "For with God nothing shall be impossible."

I remember one request very specifically. I love my parents, and I have always been so grateful for how God has used them to provide for many of my needs. I remember praying that God would give my dad a Christmas bonus. My dad has always been a hard worker and has taught my brother and me to have a good work ethic. I remember my dad working many long hours and only getting paid the bare minimum. My dad had been given some small raises throughout the years, but he had never received a Christmas bonus. Well, I prayed, believing that God would give my dad a Christmas bonus that year, and God miraculously answered that prayer. That is the one and only time that my dad ever received a Christmas bonus. God did that!

I remember my faith growing when I saw God answer specific requests. Christians, we have *power* in prayer! We need to utilize the power that God has given us. As I always like to say, "Prayer can do anything God can do, and God can do *anything!*"

George Mueller is one of those great "heroes of the faith" whom I have always admired. He saw God miraculously answer prayers daily! He saw God supply need after need after need. He also endured great trials that greatly strengthened his faith in God. He once said, "The only way to learn strong faith is to endure great trials."

Another hero of the faith I admire is Helen Keller. If God can take a girl who was not only blind, but deaf and mute, save her soul, and use her life to glorify Him, He can do anything! I cannot even imagine living in the mind of Helen. What are the odds that a child such as this would ever learn to live a normal life, let alone a fulfilled life full of God's goodness? What faith it must have taken not to live a life filled with anger and resentment that God would allow this to happen. I can only imagine that her relationship with her Savior was probably a little bit of heaven right here on this wicked earth! She once said, "True prayer brings heaven into the ordinary."

Corrie ten Boom is another great hero of the faith! How helpless she must have felt at times. She saw God's power in overwhelmingly miraculous ways! She truly realized her inabilities and allowed God to enable her. If you have never read it, you should read her story about the tissue. What a small thing to ask for, but God supplied a tissue, a ray of hope, for one of His suffering children. She explained, "When we are powerless to do a thing, it is a great joy that we can come and step inside the ability of Jesus."

When we ask God for something, how faithful He is to supply even greater and more abundantly than we could ever ask or think possible. Ephesians 3:20 says, "Now unto him that is able to do exceeding abundantly above all that we ask or think, according to the power that worketh in us".

# Having a Fruitful Prayer Life

First, you must be prepared to meet with God. The Bible talks about when we have sin in our lives, He cannot hear our prayers. "If I regard iniquity in my heart, the Lord will not hear me" (Psalm 66:18).

Thankfully, we also have 1 John 1:9, which should be memorized by every believer: "If we confess our sins, he is faithful and just to forgive us our sins, and to cleanse us from all unrighteousness." Keep a short account between you and your Savior. Confess your sins often. You never know when you are going to need to quickly get ahold of God, and if there is unconfessed sin in your life, your prayers will go no further than the ceiling above your head.

Spending time with God in prayer is so much more than just asking Him for things. I have found it best said in the words of this next song.

# *The Secret Place*

*by Cherly Reid and Ron Hamilton*

I've found a secret place
of comfort and release,
A special place of healing,
a quiet place of peace.
And everyone who dwells there
finds rest beneath God's wings.
In the shade of His pavilion,
New strength He always brings.
I find hope; I find grace
Far away from the worlds embrace.
He gives me rest; He keeps me safe;
I find His strength; I seek His face
In the secret place.
With every trial He brings,
My Lord will make a way
To strengthen and protect me,
to help me face each day.
He leads me through the valley
To draw me closer still,
Knowing even in the shadows,
I find His perfect will.
I find hope; I find grace
Far away from the worlds embrace.
He gives me rest; He keeps me safe;
I find His strength; I seek His face
In the secret place.[8]

I think it is super important to schedule a specific time and place to meet with God every day. Having a prayer journal is also very helpful when growing your prayer life. When you write down a request, you are less likely to forget it, and you can document when and how God answers.

We should also be thankful every day and for everything, even the trials and tribulations that we are sometimes faced with. I find it a blessing to set aside one day a week to be your "thankful day." This could be a day that you simply go to God and thank Him for all that you have and all that He has done for you. It is very difficult to become bitter and angry when you dwell on your blessings. How ironic that many of our greatest blessings come from our most difficult trials. I think of Ron and Shelly Hamilton and how God has used the seemingly awful situations they have experienced and turned them into fruitful lives lived for Christ. As his song says, I can most definitely see Jesus in the Hamilton family. Do others see Jesus in you?

# I Saw Jesus In You

*by Ron Hamilton*

When I enter heaven's glory
And I see my Savior's face,
I will offer Him ten thousand years of praise.
Then I'll find that special one
In whose life I saw God's Son,
And through tears of joy
with trembling lips these words I'll say:
I saw Jesus in you,
I saw Jesus in you.
I could hear His voice in the words you said
I saw Jesus in you. (Jesus in you.)
In your eyes I saw His care;
I could see His love was there.
You were faithful,
And I saw Jesus in you.
When I stand before my Father
To receive my life's reward,
And my soul is bathed in God's eternal day,
When this race on earth is run
And God sees the works I've done,
More than anything I long to hear my Father say:
I saw Jesus in you,
I saw Jesus in you.
I could hear His voice in the words you said
I saw Jesus in you. (Jesus in you.)

In your eyes I saw His care;
I could see His love was there
You were faithful
And I saw Jesus in you.[9]

[9] "I Saw Jesus in You" by Ron Hamilton, ©1994 by Majesty Music, Inc. All rights reserved; used by permission.

# Let Go and Let God

# My God Is All Knowing

God is omniscient, which means He is all knowing. He knows everything—past, present, and future. There is nothing that has or will ever happen that God did not already know about. Romans 11:33–36 says, "O the depth of the riches both of the wisdom and knowledge of God! How unsearchable are his judgements, and his ways past finding out! For who hath known the mind of our Lord? Or who hath been his counsellor? Or who hath first given to him, and it shall be recompensed unto him again? For of him, and through him, and to him, are all things: to whom be glory for ever. Amen."

God not only knows about what will transpire every second of this very day, but He knows what will transpire every second of your entire life, from the moment you were conceived until the moment that you pass from this life into the next. I am so glad that we can safely rest in Him. Did you know that God does not intend for us to fret or worry about tomorrow? Matthew 6:34 says: "Take therefore no thought for the morrow: for the morrow shall take thought for the things of itself. Sufficient unto the day is the evil thereof."

Now, this does not mean that we should not plan for the future. In fact, the Bible says that it is wise to be prudent, which means that we should act or show care and thought for the future. "I wisdom dwell with prudence …" (Proverbs 8:12a). But God gives us grace to live day by day. He does not wish for us to live or dwell in the past. He does not wish for us to live for the future. For it is today that He has put us on this earth. As Charles Spurgeon once said, "Anxiety does not empty tomorrow of its sorrows, but only empties today of its strength."

The Word of God tells us that we are not promised tomorrow. If you are a believer, then your past is under the blood. We must live for Christ today, for that may be all we have. "Go to now, ye that say, To day or to morrow we will go into such a city, and continue there a year, and buy and sell, and get gain: Whereas ye know not what shall be on the morrow. For what is your life? It is even a vapour, that appeareth for a little time, and then vanisheth away." (James 4:13–14).

Sometimes, when unexpected things arise in our lives, we often give way to worry, which means we give way to anxiety or unease. Worry is allowing one's mind to dwell on difficulties or troubles. As Christians, we must not let ourselves dwell on the difficulties or troubles of our lives; rather, we must learn to practice faith, which is putting our complete trust or confidence in God. Now, I, too, am human, and I know how difficult it is sometimes to "let go and let God," as I often hear it said. But this is a big part of spiritual growth!

# My Own Personal Experience of Letting Go and Letting God

I do my very best to be positive and upbeat, and if you asked my mother, she would describe me as an optimist, which is a person who tends to be hopeful and confident about the future or the success of something. I am often referred to as a glass-half-full kind of gal! This is no credit of my own, but is a work that God has performed within my own life. The opposite of an optimist would be a pessimist, which is a person who tends to see the worst aspect of things or believes that the worst will happen. This person is often a worrier and tends not to rest in the promises of God.

Not very long ago, it was brought to my attention that I tend to be optimistic about many areas of my life, except for one. You guessed it: that would be my marital status and, more recently, my age. Regrettably, this is an area of my life that I tend to worry about, and I often find myself trying to figure things out on my own rather than giving them to God and leaving them with Him. You could say I am somewhat of a "Negative Nancy" (sorry all you Nancys out there … you get a bad rap even if you aren't negative) about this area. It is God's will that we have faith in every area of our lives, not just most or some.

I have often viewed this with a what-did-I-do-to-deserve-this kind of attitude, which is wrong, and I have had to confess this to the Lord numerous times. God gives each of us seasons or stages in our lives, and each stage is a gift. Elisabeth Elliot says, "Single life may be only a stage of a life's journey, but even a stage is a gift. God may replace it with another gift, but the receiver accepts His gifts with thanksgiving. This gift for this day."

God has carefully planned out each stage of my life, and He has a specific time and a specific purpose for each one. I have failed miserably in this area, but praise the Lord, He has not given up on me. It may take me a very long time to learn my lesson through this, but God is so patient and so kind, and He knows! He knows what is best for us. He knows what is right for us. He knows why. He knows when. He knows how. He is *all knowing*! And I must simply put my faith and trust in Him.

# Learning to Let Go and Let God

Do you have an area in your life with which you just have a hard time putting your faith in God? Do you tend to be a worrier? It may take time, and everyone is different, but know that you can rest in Him. He cares for you and wants only what is best for you. "Casting all your care upon Him; for he careth for you" (1 Peter 5:7).

If God is all knowing, then what good does it do us to worry about something that He already has planned out? What we should do, instead, is pray about it. We should ask God for guidance and direction. Search the scriptures, and God will give you answers. Sometimes situations may seem overwhelming or daunting, but God is still on the throne. He is still God, and He is in complete control. "Be still and know that I am God" (Psalm 46:10).

Be still. Life can often get noisy, and we must purposely pause and just take a moment to quiet the noise within our souls. Get a piece of paper and write out the promises from God's Word that pertain to the specific situations you are going through at that time. I highly recommend the "Blessed Promises from Scripture" booklet, produced by Larry Stallings, that does the work for you and lists out the promises for you by category! It is simply a book of verses, or promises, from

God's Word that pertain to pretty much every situation you may be facing. It is good to know that God's Word has an answer for whatever it is that you may be going through. We must always remember to stay the course, no matter the test!

# Stay the Course

*by Megan Hamilton-Morgan and Palmer Hartsough*

I am resolved no longer to linger,
Charmed by the world's delight;
Things that are higher,
Things that are nobler
These have allured my sight.
Jesus, You are the highest and best.
I'll follow You, forsaking the rest.
I'll stay the course
no matter the test! (no matter the test!)
I am resolved to follow the Savior,
Faithful and true each day,
Heed what He says, and do what He willeth
He is the living way.
I will hasten to Him,
Hasten so glad and free.
Jesus, greatest, highest,
I willcome to Thee.,
I am resolved, and who will go with me?
Come, friends, without delay;
Taught by the Bible,
Led by the Spirit
We'll walk the Heav'nly way
Jesus, You are the highest and best.
I'll follow You, forsaking the rest.
I'll stay the course, no matter the test! (no matter the test!)
No matter the test![10]

---

# Overcoming Fear

# My God Is All Powerful

God is omnipotent, which means that He has unlimited power and there is *nothing* too hard for Him to do! Wow, what a mighty God we serve! How wonderful it would be if we as Christians really grasped the magnitude of this promise. "Ah Lord God! Behold, thou hast made the heaven and the earth by thy great power and stretched out arm, and there is nothing too hard for thee" (Jeremiah 32:17).

If we truly grasped the truth that God is all-powerful, then why in the world would we ever experience *fear*? Fear is crippling to a Christian. The definition of fear is an unpleasant emotion caused by belief that someone or something is dangerous, likely to cause pain, or a threat. Did you know that fear does not come from God? "For God hath not given us the spirit of fear; but of power, and of love, and of a sound mind" (2 Timothy 1:7).

Fear comes directly from Satan. If you have accepted Christ as your Savior, your fate is sealed; but you had better believe that Satan will do everything in his power to destroy your life and prevent you from being a victorious Christian and an effective witness for Him. Satan's goal is to destroy you, to destroy your testimony, and to prevent you from being used by God. Fear is often an effective tool that Satan uses to paralyze believers and brand them as useless for Christ. "Be sober, be vigilant; because your adversary the devil, as a roaring lion, walketh about, seeking whom he may devour" (1 Peter 5:8).

Fear often prevents the Christian from speaking out for Christ. It is like a poisonous venom that halts Christians from being used by God. God gives us power, love, and sound minds. Ultimately, God is all-powerful and can help us overcome the fears that Satan sets before us as roadblocks to prevent the furtherance of the gospel.

# My Own Experience of Overcoming Fear

Fear is one of those four-letter words, and unfortunately, Satan has used it many times in my life. I wish I could say that I have gotten complete victory over the power of fear, but this is an ongoing process and sometimes a daily battle for me.

For instance, since I was a little girl, I have loved to sing. Singing was fun for me as a child, and I enjoyed getting up in front of people to sing songs and praise the Lord! I still loved to sing as I got older, but fear became a very real roadblock for me when I was asked to get up in front of a crowd of people. I still had a desire to sing and use my talents for the Lord, but fear often kept me from fulfilling that desire. In fact, there was a large portion of my life when I did not sing in church at all. Fear kept me from doing what I knew God wanted me to do. It was not until the last few years that I have allowed God to help me slowly overcome my fear of singing in front of people. As Elisabeth Elliot once said, "Sometimes fear does not subside, and one must choose to do it *afraid*."

Fear also almost kept me from doing God's will and going to a Christian college. I was homeschooled from sixth through twelfth grade, and I was not used to being in a traditional classroom setting or around many people. The simple thought of having to take freshman speech made my mouth go dry and my heart palpitate. I'm not kidding; these types of situations petrified me, but God began working in my heart and growing my desire to attend a Christian college, so off I went. Was I afraid? Yes, very much so—but I knew that was what God wanted me to do, and again, I went even though I was afraid. God gave me what I needed to accomplish each task, one at a time. The day I graduated was a great testament of God's omnipotence. Elisabeth Elliot says, "The heart set to do the Father's will, need never fear defeat."

I also recall a time that I helped minister in a small local Bible club. I enjoyed sitting with the kids, playing games with them, and helping with craft time, but when I was asked to present the Bible lesson, I was terrified. What if I didn't get the point across correctly? What if someone asked a question that I did not know? What if I forgot something, what if … what if … what if? Well, I agreed to present the lesson, but with great fear in my heart. You know, Satan is not only the one who brings fear, but he also brings a lot of what-ifs. I remember calling my mom and asking her to pray with me for God to calm my fears, for the kids to sit still and listen, and for there not to be any distractions. God performed a miracle that day. I went up to give the lesson, and God calmed my fears, prevented distractions, and spoke through me that day. That was not me; that was *all God*! When we try to do a thing in our own strength, we will fail miserably; but if we allow Him, He can do great things through us, for His glory! As Elisabeth Elliot says, "Fear arises when we imagine that everything depends on us."

One of the biggest lessons I continue to learn is that I, myself, cannot do the work of God. I must surrender myself and allow God to do His work through me. I must make myself available but trying to do anything in my own strength will always end in failure. Do I still become afraid? Yes, but I am continuously learning how to step out in faith and let God do the work through me.

# Experiencing God's Power through Overcoming Fear

When I look back now, I can see God's hand in many moments where He calmed my fears and gave me the confidence to overcome these obstacles, one at a time. There is a fun song called "Little by Little," written by Ron Hamilton, that explains this process very well.

# Little by Little

by Ron Hamilton

When mountains tower rugged and high,
Rise to the challenge,
Look to the sky.
Trust in the Lord
And start up to climb,
Reach for the goal one step at a time.
Little by little, inch by inch;
By the yard it's hard,
By the inch what a synch;
Never stare up the stairs,
just step up the steps;
Little by little, inch by inch.
Growing in Christ takes work every day,
Reading your Bible, learning to pray.
Build Godly habits, seek help divine.
Great things are done
One step at a time.
Little by little, inch by inch;
By the yard it's hard,
by the inch what a synch;
Never stare up the stairs,
just step up the steps;
Little by little, inch by inch.
What a synch![11]

[11] "Little by Little" by Ron Hamilton, ©1987 by Majesty Music, Inc. All rights reserved; used by permission.

There are so many simple truths in this song. God may have something big He wants you to do, and looking at the entire daunting task might very well bring an overwhelming sense of fear. Take it one step at a time and ask God to help you accomplish each step. He will give you the grace and strength needed to accomplish such tasks and will deliver you from the bondage of fear.

We serve a mighty God! We need not fear people or worry about what could or might happen. You must fix your eyes on Him. Listen to His still, small voice and follow His lead, and He will use you to accomplish many great things for His glory! There is none greater than my God! My God is a God of wonders, and His wonders are displayed throughout every generation!

# God of Wonders

## by Adam Morgan

Who is like unto the Lord most high?
Who filled the seas
And formed the skies.
Who walks upon the wings of the wind.
Whose thoughts no man can comprehend.
Through ev'ry generation
His Wonders are displayed
From forming all creation
to freeing those enslaved!
God of Wonders
Who reigns victorious.
God of wonders, enthroned in praise.
All earth trembles
Before His presence.
God of wonders the Ancient of Days.
Who has heard His mighty works of old,
Of Noah's Flood, of Jericho,
Of taming mighty lions in the den,
Of Egypt's plagues, Goliath's end?
Through ev'ry generation
His wonders are displayed
From forming all creation
to freeing those enslaved!
God of wonders
Who reigns victorious.
God of wonders, enthroned in praise.
All earth trembles

Before His presence.
God of wonders, the Ancient of Days.
Who is like unto the Lord Most High?
The Lord most high?[12]

*Joy*

*Unspeakable*

*and Full*

*of Glory*

# My God Is Steadfast, Unchangeable

To be steadfast means to be resolutely (in an admirably purposeful, determined, and unwavering manner) or dutifully (in a conscientious or obedient manner) firm and unwavering. That is my God, Steadfast! "Jesus Christ the same yesterday, and to day, and for ever" (Hebrews 13:8).

Unchangeable means to be *not* liable to variation or *able* to be altered. I may go through many changes, but my God is Unchangeable! "For I am the Lord, I change not" (Malachi 3:6a).

There are many things that come to mind when considering God's steadfastness, but one of the most unique things that I think of is the *joy* He gives to those who believe in Him. Did you know that spiritual joy, or joy given by God, lasts forever? The joy of His salvation is eternal, but He also wants to give us daily joy, which develops when we faithfully walk with Him, we contentedly rest in Him, and we daily grow in our spiritual walks with Him! Joy is a part of the fruit of the Spirit. The fruit of the Spirit is the characteristics that develop in a Christian's life through spiritual growth. "But the fruit of the Spirit is love, joy, peace, longsuffering, gentleness, goodness, faith, meekness, temperance: against such there is no law" (Galatians 5:22–23).

The stronger our relationships are with our Savior, the more joy we will have in our day-to-day lives. Joy is something that we must choose, sometimes daily. Joy is not merely happiness. You see, happiness depends on happenings, and many things that happen in our lives may leave us unhappy; however, joy is something that we as Christians can and should possess even amid sadness, sickness, trials, tragedies, and all of life's hard times. I guess that is why I think of joy when I think of unwavering. Our joy in the Lord should be unwavering, steadfast, unchangeable. "For the joy of the Lord is your strength" (Nehemiah 8:10c).

It is the joy of the Lord from which we gain the daily strength to endure hardships. We can either choose to have joy or to live in our own strength. We can choose to trust God and obtain joy, or we can doubt and lose our joy. God is more than capable of caring for our needs, and when we rest in His ability to do so, we can have joy and peace in our hearts, even amid the most trying of times. Kay Warren says, "Joy is the settled assurance that God is in control of all the details of my life, the quiet confidence that ultimately everything is going to be alright, and the determined choice to praise God in every situation."

# My Own Experience of Choosing Joy Amid the Hard Times

The most miserable person on earth is the Christian who is outside of God's will. There are many things in my life that have turned out differently than how I would have planned them. There have been seasons of my life when I was angry at God, I was discouraged and downtrodden, I wanted to give up, and I had simply lost my joy.

The year I turned twenty-nine was a very difficult year for me. I felt as if God had forgotten all about me. I was simply devastated that I was about to start a new decade of my life alone. I had to learn that I was never alone. God was right there beside me every step of the way, and He was growing me and teaching me to trust Him through this trying time. He was patient with me, and He never gave up on me.

In my early to mid-thirties, I found myself almost wandering from place to place. I was not content, and I kept trying to find happiness instead of resting in the joy of the Lord. My faith was little, and my trust was slim. Through a series of difficult circumstances, I felt hurt and abandoned. It was most difficult to be joyful while watching others live out the lives that I had always dreamed of. I felt that there was no one who could possibly understand or who even cared about the hurt and pain that I was feeling. But God—God knew. He understood, He cared, and He has a special plan for me and my life. He saw me, felt my pain, and saw the tears. He was there; He didn't change, and He steadfastly waited for me to accept the comfort and joy that He had to offer. Charles Spurgeon once said, "God is too wise to be mistaken. God is too good to be unkind. And, when you can't trace His hand, you can always trust His heart."

Believe me, there were many times that I thought for sure God was mistaken. But He, in His infinite wisdom, knew what was best for me and what I needed in that very difficult season of my life. There were times that I doubted God's goodness because I thought He was deliberately withholding something good from me that I so desperately desired. There are still days when I can't always trace His hand, but through it all, I have learned that, despite everything, I can—and must—always trust His heart. There is a very real joy and contentment when you put your unknown future into the hands of your known, steadfast, and unchangeable God and rest in the truth that God is in control. He has a purpose and a plan, and He will never forget or abandon His children.

# Experiencing His Joy, Unspeakable and Full of Glory

Experiencing the joy of the Lord is truly unspeakable (not able to be expressed in words) and is full of glory. We must take the time to slow down, to quiet the noisiness of the soul, and just simply linger in His presence. Allow God to develop the fruit of the Spirit within you and change you into His likeness and into His image. Romans 12:2 says, "And be not conformed to this world: but be ye transformed by the renewing of your mind, that ye may prove what is that good, and acceptable, and perfect, will of God."

Joy also comes when we serve others. Our human nature will always want to put ourselves first, but if we want true joy, we must put *Jesus* first, then *others,* and then *yourself.* John 15:11 says, "These things have I spoken unto you, that my joy might remain in you, and that your joy might be full."

We must grow in the Lord daily. Make time to grow your relationship with Him. He is always the same. He never changes. His love is forever, and He knows my name.

# Always the Same

by Ron Hamilton

I am His, He is mine;
Jesus knows my name.
I can rest in His arms;
He's always the same.
When I fall, when I call,
Jesus takes my hand.
Cleansing me, lifting me,
He helps me to stand.
Always the same,
O praise His name!
Jesus never changes;
He's always the same.
Always together,
His love is forever.
Jesus never changes;
He's always the same.
In His love I'm secure;
We shall never part.
In His Word I will trust
And give Him all my heart.
In the dark of the night,
When my heart would fear,
Lovingly, tenderly,
My Savior is near.
Always the same,
O praise His name!
Jesus never changes;
He's always the same.

Always together,
His love is forever.
Jesus never changes,
He's always the same.[13]

# I Surrender All

# My God Is My Everything—
# Total Surrender

Is God truly number one in your life? Many times, we say that He is, but is He really? Has there ever been a specific time in your Christian life that you have completely surrendered yourself to God? You surrender your heart to Him when you accept Him as your Savior, but have you surrendered your life to Him, your will to Him, your dreams to Him, and your desires to Him? Then said Jesus unto his disciples, If any man will come after me, let him deny himself, and take up his cross, and follow me. For whosoever will save his life shall lose it: and whosoever will lose his life for my sake shall find it. For what is a man profited, if he shall gain the whole world, and lose his own soul? Or what shall a man give in exchange for his soul? For the Son of man shall come in the glory of his Father with his angels; and then he shall reward every man according to his works. (Matthew 16:24–27)

The victorious Christian life requires that we "die" to self daily. We still have that old sense of self—our old nature—within us, and we must fight the temptations of the devil daily. "I am crucified with Christ: nevertheless I live; yet not I, but Christ liveth in me: and the life which I now live in the flesh I live by the faith of the Son of God, who loved me, and gave himself for me" (Galatians 2:20).

The victorious Christian life requires complete and total *surrender.* To completely surrender requires a humble heart and a teachable spirit. Give your life to God, and He will do a work that you never thought possible. The world and Satan offer things that look pretty on the outside, but they will turn around and consume you and destroy you. Give your life to God completely and wholly, and He will transform you into His image. "I beseech you therefore, brethren, by the mercies of God, that ye present your bodies a living sacrifice, holy, acceptable unto God, which is your reasonable service. And be not conformed to this world: but be ye transformed by the renewing of your mind, that ye may prove what is that good, and acceptable, and perfect, will of God" (Romans 12:1–2).

# My Own Experience of Complete Surrender

I remember one time in my life, while at college, during an invitation, that we were all asked to step out and come forward if we were willing to surrender our lives to do whatever it was that God wanted us to do. I recall stepping forward, but I knew in my heart that it was a halfhearted surrender. I felt like I still had some things in my life that I wanted to control. I wanted to do God's will, but I wanted to do it my own way. God had many lessons for me to learn to get to the place where I was willing to surrender everything to Him.

I picture my heart kind of like a house. It has windows and doors, closets, bedrooms, an office, and so on. I let God into the main house, even into the bedrooms and the office, but I had one or two closets and a couple of drawers that I kept shut and wouldn't let God be in complete control of. You will find out very quickly that if you want God to fulfill His perfect purpose in your life, you must surrender every square inch of your heart to Him. You must realize that there is nothing good in you, but it is Him in us that does the work. We must yield our lives as empty vessels and allow Him to reign in every area of our lives.

Some people view complete surrender to the Lord as a life sentence or a lifeless, unhappy way to live. That could not be further from the truth. I remember always thinking that if I completely surrendered my life to the Lord, He would send me to some remote country where I did not want to go, and I would have to do and eat things that I did not want to. My friend, God calls some to be missionaries, some to be pastors, some to be mothers, some to be church secretaries, and even some to be those sitting quietly behind the scenes, faithfully praying for those whom He has called to go! Whatever God has for you will always be more fulfilling and satisfying than anything you and I could ever imagine for ourselves. The peace that overflows your soul with knowing that you are in God's complete and perfect will and that He is using you for the purpose that He created you is like nothing else you will ever experience.

Little by little, I began to surrender those things that I was holding on to. I truly believe that I am now at a place in my life where I have laid my all on the alter. I still feel that I am being prepared, and though I am not completely sure what exactly I am being prepared for, I have full confidence that God will fulfill the perfect purpose for which He placed me here on this earth. I may not know exactly how or when, but I have surrendered my everything to Him, and I plan to let Him reveal the details in His perfect timing.

As Elisabeth Elliot said, "To love God is to love His will. It is to be content with His timing and wise appointment."

# Surrender Your All to God

To surrender is to cease resistance, to submit to. Is there any area of your life that you are holding on to or resisting? Give it to God! Give it all to God! Completely surrender to Him and allow Him to do a mighty work in your life.

My God is my salvation, and my eternity is secure in Him. My God is my Creator, and I know that I am fearfully and wonderfully made. My God is my sustainer, and I can always find hope in Him. My God is my friend and comforter, and I need never be lonely. My God is good and only good, and I need never doubt His goodness. My God is all knowing, and I need not worry about tomorrow. My God is all powerful, and I need never fear. My God is steadfast, unchangeable, and my joy comes from Him. My God is my everything; He is absolutely everything that I could ever want, need, or desire.

Surrender your all to Him, and you will see how truly amazing He really is!

# Here's My Everything

by Rachel McCutcheon

You formed me with your Holy hands
before my birth.
You planned your perfect purpose
for me on this earth.
I want to be all that You've
created me to be;
And for all you've done,
you deserve the Glory.

Here's my Everything!
I give you every part of me.
I Surrender,
my plans my hopes my dreams.
You're so amazing!
Makes me wish I had more to bring
But if you'll take it,
Here's my everything.

Lately I've been learning
More about your love.
And finding for my every need
It is enough.
Though I'm never more aware
of my own unworthiness,
Then when I come and
Bow before your holiness.

Here's my everything.
I give you every part of me.
I Surrender,

My plans my hopes my dreams.
You're so amazing!
Makes me wish I had more to bring
But if you'll take it,
here's my everything!

I have nothing I can boast of
And if there's any good in me,
It's all because of you Lord.
So, I pledge my offering.

Here's my everything!
I give you every part of me.
I Surrender,
my plans my hopes my dreams.
You're so amazing!
Makes me wish I had more to bring
But if you'll take it,
here's my everything.
You're so AMAZING![14]

---

# Section 3: How Can I Know God and Know God?

The answer is simple, really: you must first know Him as your personal Lord and Savior by accepting His payment for your sins. At the point of salvation, you enter a personal relationship with Him. If you also want to know Him, you must then grow your relationship with Him by learning about Him in His Word, by leaning on Him and His precious promises, by walking with Him daily, and by surrendering yourself to Him through every step of this earthly journey. Salvation is simple and happens in an instant, but getting to know God is a lifelong process that will continue into eternity. Oh, that we may know Him better, day by day and moment by moment!

# Day by Day

by Lina Sandell

Day by day and with each passing moment,
Strength I find to meet my trials here;
Trusting in my Father's wise bestowment,
I've no cause for worry or for fear.
He whose heart is kind beyond all measure
Gives unto each day what He deems best—
Lovingly, it's part of pain and pleasure,
Mingling toil with peace and rest.
Every day the Lord Himself is near me
With a special mercy for each hour;
All my cares He fain would bear, and cheer me,
He whose name is Counselor and Pow'r.
The protection of His child and treasure
Is a charge that on Himself He laid;
"As thy days, thy strength shall be in measure,"
This the pledge to me He made.

Help me then in every tribulation
So to trust Thy promises, O Lord,
That I lose not faith's sweet consolation
Offered me within Thy holy Word.
Help me, Lord, when toil and trouble meeting,
E'er to take, as from a father's hand,
One by one, the days, the moments fleeting
Till I reach the promised land.

# Conclusion

If there is only one thing you take away from this book, I pray that it is to know that God is all you will ever need. If you give your life to God, He will bless you more abundantly than you could ever think or imagine. He truly is amazing! Talk to Him, walk with Him, listen to Him, and follow Him! He has promised never to leave us nor forsake us. Put God first in your life, and everything else will fall right into place. C.T. Studd said, "Only one life, 'twill soon be past, only what's done for Christ will last."

In the end, there is nothing to show for a life lived for self and the flesh. This life is so short; surrender to God, and He will give you something that will last through eternity! "But seek ye first the kingdom of God, and his righteousness; and all these things shall be added unto you" (Matthew 6:33).

Put God first in your life. Live fully for Him, and He will bless you more abundantly than you could ever think or imagine. "Lay not up for yourselves treasures upon earth, where moth and rust doth corrupt, and where thieves break through and steal: But lay up for yourselves treasures in heaven, where neither moth nor rust doth corrupt, and where thieves do not break through nor steal: For where your treasure is, there will your heart be also" (Matthew 6:19–20).

The "things" that we would consider treasures on this earth are nothing in comparison with the treasures that we can store up in heaven, our eternal home. The souls of people, the investments made in the lives of others, the time and energy spent ministering to others—these are the things that please God and will never be forgotten throughout eternity! "Love not the world, neither the things that are in the world. If any man love the world, the love of the Father is not in him. For all that is in the world, the lust of the flesh, and the lust of the eyes, and the pride of life, is not of the Father, but is of the world. And the world passeth away, and the lust thereof: but he that doeth the will of God abideth for ever" (1 John 2:15–17).

Printed in the United States
by Baker & Taylor Publisher Services